ONE-POT

D1556046

Colofon

© 2002 Rebo International b.v., Lisse, The Netherlands

www.rebo-publishers.com - info@rebo-publishers.com

This 2nd edition reprinted 2004

Original recipes and photographs: © R&R Publishing Pty. Ltd.

Design, editing and production: Minkowsky Graphics, Enkhuizen, The Netherlands

Translation and adaptation: American Pie, London, UK and Sunnyvale, California, USA

ISBN 90 366 1476 7

All rights reserved.

ONE-POT

a wealth of flavors combined into

creative cooking

REBO
PUBLISHERS

Foreword

The most special characteristic of one-pot meals is that the flavors of the different

ingredients all influence each other. This can result in unique fusions and culinary

masterpieces. For all fans of one-dish meals this book contains a very special

collection of recipes for foods that are slow-cooked in a Dutch oven, casserole,

or deep pot. From a classic dish such as Ratatouille in Fresh Tomato Sauce to an

Exotic Lamb Casserole with Couscous and Fish Casserole with Rosemary-flavored

Mashed Potatoes there are plenty of delicious ideas. Grab the pan, while I just

step out to the store.

Abbreviations

tbsp = tablespoon

tsp = teaspoon

g = gram

kg = kilogram

fl oz = fluid ounce

lb = pound

oz = ounce

ml = milliliter

l = liter

°C = degree Celsius

°F = degree Fahrenheit

Where three measurements are given, the

first is the American cup measure.

1. Heat the butter in a large frying pan and cook the onions and pork over medium heat for 5 minutes. Add apples, herbs, broth, and black pepper to taste, bring to the boil, then reduce heat and simmer for 1 hour or until pork is tender. Using a slotted spoon, remove pork and set aside.

2. Push liquid and solids through a sieve and return to pan with the pork.

3. To make the sauce, melt the butter in a frying pan and cook apple over a medium heat for 2 minutes. Stir in chives and tomatoes and bring to the boil, reduce heat, and simmer for 5 minutes. Pour into pan with pork and cook over a medium heat for 5 minutes longer. Just prior to serving, sprinkle with cracked black peppercorns.

Ingredients

1oz/30g butter

2 onions, chopped

1 lb/500g lean diced pork

3 large apples, peeled,
cored and chopped

1 tbsp/15g dried mixed herbs

3 cups/24fl oz/750ml chicken broth

freshly ground black pepper

Apple sauce

1oz/30g butter

2 apples, peeled, cored and chopped

2 tbsp/30g snipped fresh chives

1¾ cups/440g/14oz canned tomatoes,
undrained and mashed

1 tsp/5g cracked black peppercorns

Apple Pork Casserole

one-pot

1. Trim meat of all visible fat. Heat 2 tbsp/30ml oil in a large saucepan. Cook the meat in batches until well browned on all sides. Transfer to a plate and set aside.

2. Heat remaining oil and cook onion and bell pepper for 2-3 minutes or until onion softens. Stir in tomato paste and broth. Stir well to lift pan sediment.

3. Add cardamom, cinnamon and bell pepper. Bring to the boil, reduce heat and simmer for 5 minutes. Return meat to the pan with coriander. Cover and simmer for 1½ hours or until meat is tender and sauce thickens

Athenian **Lamb Hotpot**

Ingredients

2 lb/1 kg boneless lamb, cubed

3 tbsp olive oil

2 onions, finely chopped

1 green bell pepper (pepper), seeded and chopped

8 fl oz/250ml tomato paste

6 fl oz/185ml chicken broth

½ tsp ground cardamom

1 large cinnamon stick

freshly ground black pepper

2 tbsp chopped fresh coriander

one-pot

1. Heat the oil in a large, heavy-based saucepan. Add the onions and garlic and fry for 6-8 minutes, until golden. Add the pears and fry for a further 6-8 minutes, until the pears soften and start to brown, stirring and scraping the bottom of the pan occasionally. Add a little water if the mixture becomes too dry.

2. Stir in the tomato paste and curry powder and fry for 1–2 minutes to release the flavors. Add the broth, season, and bring to the boil. Reduce the heat and simmer, uncovered, for 15 minutes or until the liquid has slightly reduced.

3. Add the carrots, cover, then simmer for 5 minutes. Add the broccoli and cauliflower, cover the pan, then simmer for a further 10-15 minutes, or until the vegetables are tender. Sprinkle with the coriander just before serving.

Ingredients

3 tbsp/45ml groundnut oil

2 onions, finely chopped

6 cloves garlic, minced

2 pears, peeled, cored, and finely chopped

3 tbsp/45ml tomato paste

2 tbsp/50g mild curry powder

2½ cups/1 pint/600ml vegetable broth

salt and black pepper

7oz/200g baby carrots

1 cup/8oz/250g broccoli flowerets

9oz/250g baby cauliflower, quartered

3 tbsp/45g chopped fresh coriander

Baby Vegetable Curry with Pears

1. Cover beans with cold water and soak overnight. Drain and rinse.

2. In a large soup pot, combine beans with water, chorizo, salt pork, onion, garlic, parsley, bayleaf, pepper, and cumin. In a small cup, mix together oil and paprika until smooth then stir into the pot. Bring to the boil, cover, and simmer 2 hours, or until beans are tender. Add salt to taste. Turn off the heat and let stew stand 20 minutes to thicken, then reheat. Serve in soup bowls. Add a piece of chorizo and salt pork to each serving.

Bean Stew with Chorizo

Ingredients

2 cups/1 lb/455g white haricot or navy beans

5 cups/2 pints/1.25 l water

4oz/115g chorizo

4oz/115g salt pork or slab bacon,

cut in 1in/2½cm cubes

1 small onion, chopped

4 cloves garlic

2 tbsp/50g minced parsley

1 bayleaf

freshly ground pepper

¼ tsp/1.25g ground cumin

1 tbsp/15ml olive oil

1 tsp/5g paprika

salt

1. Heat oil in large heavy based saucepan. Cook onions over medium heat until golden. Stir in allspice, cinnamon, ginger, and bell pepper.

2. Add meat to pan, and cook over high heat until browned. Stir in lemongrass and chicken broth. Bring to the boil, reduce heat, and simmer, covered, for 45 minutes.

3. Stir in pumpkin, cover, and simmer for 45 minutes or until beef is tender. Remove from heat and stir in garlic. Season to taste.

Note:

Serve this unusual and flavorful dish accompanied by bowls of plain yogurt and topped with freshly chopped coriander (cilantro).

Ingredients

2 tbsp/30ml oil

2 onions, chopped

1 tsp/5g whole allspice

1 cinnamon stick

1 tsp/5g grated fresh ginger

2 green bell peppers, sliced

1½ lb/750g chuck steak, cut into 2in/5cm cubes

Beef with Pumpkin and Lemongrass

2 tbsp chopped fresh lemongrass

2 cups/16fl oz/500ml chicken broth

2 cups/1 lb/500g pumpkin, peeled, cut into 1½in/4cm cubes

2 cloves garlic, crushed

one-pot

1. To make filling, toss meat in flour to coat. Shake off excess flour.
   Melt butter and oil in a large heavy-based saucepan and cook meat in batches for 3-4 minutes or until browned. Remove meat from pan and set aside.

2. Add onions and garlic to pan and cook over a medium heat for 3–4 minutes or until onion softens. Stir in mushrooms and cook for 2 minutes longer. Combine wine and broth, pour into pan, and cook for 4-5 minutes, stirring constantly and scraping sediment from the pan. Bring to the boil, then reduce heat. Return meat to pan with bayleaf, parsley, Worcestershire sauce, and black pepper. Cover and simmer for 1½ hours or until meat is tender. Stir in cornstarch mixture and cook, stirring, until liquid thickens. Remove pan from heat and leave to cool.

3. To make the dough, place butter and lard in a bowl and mix well. Cover and refrigerate until firm. Sift the flour into a large mixing bowl. Cut one-quarter of butter mixture into small pieces and rub into flour using fingertips until mixture resembles coarse bread crumbs. Mix in enough water to form a firm dough.

4. Turn dough onto a floured surface and knead lightly. Roll dough out to a 6x10in/15x25cm rectangle. Cut another one-quarter of butter mixture into small pieces and place over top two-thirds of pastry. Fold the bottom third of pastry up and top third of dough down to give three even layers. Half-turn dough to have open end facing you and roll out to a rectangle. Repeat folding and rolling twice. Cover dough and refrigerate for 1 hour.

5. Place cooled filling in a 1¼ cup/10oz/300g oval pie dish. On a lightly floured surface, roll out pastry 1½in/4cm larger than pie dish. Cut off a ½in/1cm strip from edge of the dough. Brush rim of dish with water and press dough strip onto rim. Brush pastry strip with water.
   Lift pastry top over filling and press gently to seal edges.
   Trim and knock back edges to make a decorative edge.
   Brush with egg and bake for 30 minutes.

Beef and Mushroom Pie

Ingredients

9oz/250g packaged puff dough

3oz/90g butter, softened

3oz/90g lard, softened

2 cups/16oz/250g all-purpose flour

½ cup/4 fl oz/125ml cold water

Beef and mushroom filling

2lb/900g lean beef, cut into 1in/2½cm cubes

½ cup/60g seasoned all-purpose flour

3oz/60g butter

3 tbsp olive oil

2 onions, chopped

2 cloves garlic, crushed

1 cup/8oz/250g button mushrooms, sliced

½ cup/4fl oz/125ml red wine

1½cup/4fl oz/125ml beef broth

1 bayleaf, 2 tbsp/60ml minced parsley

1 tbsp/15ml Worcestershire sauce

freshly ground black pepper

1 tbsp/15g cornstarch mixed with

   2 tbsp/30ml water

1 egg, lightly beaten

1. Soak the sliced ginger and finely shredded green onions (scallions) in the water.

2. In a bowl, combine the pork and drained crabmeat. Slice the green onions (scallions) into quarters lengthwise then chop them. Extract about 1 tbsp/15ml juice from the ginger by pressing it in a garlic crusher and mix it with the pork and crabmeat. Add salt and cornstarch and knead well by hand. Divide mixture into 4 large balls. Deep-fry in oil over medium heat until golden-brown.

3. Quickly sauté bok choy in 3 tbsp/45ml oil. Remove and place in a lightly greased pottery casserole or a deep, heavy, lidded saucepan. Place meatballs on top of bok choy, sprinkle sherry over them. Mix sugar and soy sauce with the broth and add it. Cover and cook on stove top on high for 15 minutes then reduce heat and simmer on low for about 45 minutes. Alternatively, place casserole in a hot oven and reduce it to low for the same period.

Ingredients

2in/5cm ginger root, thinly sliced

4 shredded green onions

1¾ cups/14oz/400g lean ground pork

½ cup/4oz/115g can crabmeat

pinch of salt

Beijing Pork and Crab Meatball Stew

1 tbsp/15g cornstarch

oil for deep-frying

4 bok choy leaves, cut in half lengthwise

1 tbsp/15ml dry sherry

¼ cup/2fl oz/60ml water

3 cups/24 fl oz/750ml broth

2 tsp/10g sugar

2 tbsp/30ml soy sauce

one-pot

1. Heat 1 tbsp/15g of the oil with half the butter in a large frying pan. Add the onions, celery, carrots, and garlic. Cook for 10 minutes, stirring often. Season, remove from the pan and set aside.

2. Preheat the oven to 400°F/200°C. Heat 1 tbsp/15ml of oil in the pan, add the mushrooms, peppers, oregano, and thyme and cook for 5 minutes, stirring often. Season and add to the other vegetables. Heat the remaining oil and fry the eggplant for 3 minutes, turning once, to brown.

3. Grease a lasagne dish with the rest of the butter. Add the vegetables, pour in the broth, and loosely cover with foil. Cook for 40 minutes. Remove the foil, stir and cook for a further 5 minutes or until tender.

4. Meanwhile, make the dough crust.

   Sift the flour and baking powder into a bowl. Rub in the butter, until the texture resembles coarse bread crumbs. Mix in the cheddar, bread crumbs, cream, parsley, and oregano, and season to taste. Increase the oven temperature to 450°F/230°C. Spoon the crust mixture over the vegetables. Cook for 20 minutes or until golden. Set aside to rest for 10 minutes before serving.

Braised Vegetables with a Cheddar Crust

Ingredients

4 tbsp/60ml olive oil

1oz/25g butter

2 red onions, thinly sliced

1 head celery, thickly sliced

2 large carrots, thickly sliced

2 cloves garlic, crushed

salt and black pepper

4 large cup mushrooms, sliced

3 red bell peppers, deseeded and cut into strips

1 tsp/5g each dried oregano and thyme

2 eggplant (aubergines), thickly sliced

1¼ cups/½ pint/300ml vegetable broth

For the crust

2 cups/8oz/225g all-purpose (plain) flour

2 tsp/10g baking powder

6 tbsp/3oz/75g chilled butter, cubed

3oz/75g cheddar cheese, grated

2 tbsp/30 fresh bread crumbs

⅓ cup/3½fl oz/100ml heavy (double) cream

2 tbsp/50g minced fresh parsley

1 tsp/5g dried oregano

1. Wash rabbit and pat dry. Cut into serving pieces. Season with salt and pepper. Heat oil or butter in a large, lidded frying pan or saucepan. Add rabbit pieces and quickly brown all sides on high heat.

2. Remove to a plate. Reduce heat, add onions and cook until golden. Add water and stir to dislodge sediment and mix pan juices. Return rabbit to the pan, sprinkle with the chopped thyme and add bayleaves. Cover and simmer for 40 minutes.

Ingredients

3lb 5oz/1.5 kg rabbit pieces

salt and pepper

2 tbsp/30ml oil or 2 tbsp/1oz/30g clarified butter

6 small onions, halved

2 cups/16fl oz/500ml water

Braised Rabbit with Dried Fruits

1 tbsp chopped, fresh thyme

2 bayleaves

1 scant cup/7oz/200g dried mixed fruits

⅔ cup/5½ fl oz/150ml red wine

⅔ cup/5½ fl oz/150ml single (light) cream

one-pot

1. Cut each chicken thigh into 4 pieces. Heat the oil in a large, heavy-based frying pan and add the peppers, onion, ginger, garlic, spices, and a large pinch of salt. Fry over a low heat for 5 minutes or until the peppers and onion have softened.

2. Add the chicken and 2 tbsp/30ml of the yogurt. Increase the heat to medium and cook for 4 minutes or until the yogurt is absorbed.

    Repeat with the rest of the yogurt.

3. Increase the heat to high, stir in the tomatoes and 1 scant cup/7fl oz/200ml water and bring to the boil.

    Reduce the heat, cover, and simmer for 30 minutes or until the chicken is tender, stirring occasionally and adding more water if the sauce becomes too dry.

4. Uncover the pan, increase the heat to high and cook, stirring constantly, for 5 minutes or until the sauce thickens. Garnish with coriander (cilantro) sprigs.

Chicken Rogan Josh

Ingredients

8 skinless boneless chicken thighs

1 tbsp/15ml vegetable oil

1 small red bell pepper and 1 small green bell pepper, deseeded and thinly sliced

1 onion, thinly sliced

2in/5cm piece of fresh root ginger, finely chopped

2 cloves garlic, crushed

2 tbsp/30g garam masala

1 tsp/5g each paprika, turmeric, and chili powder

4 cardamom pods, crushed

large pinch of salt

1 scant cup/7fl oz/200ml Greek-style yogurt

1¾ cups/14 oz/400g can chopped tomatoes

fresh coriander to garnish

1. To toast the cashews, spread nuts over a baking tray and bake in the oven at 350°F/180°C for 5-10 minutes or until lightly and evenly browned. Toss back and forth occasionally with a spoon to ensure even browning. Alternatively, place nuts under a medium-hot broiler and cook, tossing back and forth until roasted.

2. Melt ghee or butter in a saucepan over a medium heat, add garlic and onions and cook, stirring, for 3 minutes or until onions are golden.

3. Stir in curry paste, coriander, and nutmeg and cook for 2 minutes or until fragrant. Add chicken and cook, stirring, for 5 minutes or until chicken is brown.

4. Add cashews, cream, and coconut milk, bring to the boil. Reduce heat and simmer, stirring occasionally, for 40 minutes or until chicken is tender.

Ingredients

2 tbsp/2oz/60g cashews, toasted and ground

4 tbsp/2oz/60g ghee or butter

2 cloves garlic, crushed

2 onions, minced

1 tbsp/15ml curry paste

1 tbsp/15g ground coriander

Cashew Nut Butter **Chicken**

½ tsp/2.5g ground nutmeg

1½ lb/750g boneless chicken thigh or breast

fillets, cut into ¾in/2cm cubes

1¼ cups/10fl oz/315ml heavy (double) cream

2 tbsp/50ml coconut milk

1. Combine marinade ingredients and add pork, stirring so pork is completely covered. Marinate for at least 2 hours.

2. Heat oil in a heavy-based pan and add pork cubes, turning to sear all sides. Drain off any oil, add coconut milk, and bring almost to the boil. Reduce heat, skim the surface, and simmer, covered, for about 45 minutes, or until tender.

3. Peel the hard-boiled eggs, add to pan, and cook for about 10 minutes. Serve garnished with the 3 green onions (scallions) cut into narrow 2in/5cm strips and the beansprouts. Sprinkle with the nuoc mam (Vietnamese fish sauce).

Coconut Pork Stew

Ingredients

2½ lb/1kg lean boneless pork, cut into large cubes

4 tbsp/60ml vegetable oil

2½ cups/ coconut milk

6 hard-boiled eggs

3 green onions (scallions)

½ cup/4oz/125g beansprouts

4 tbsp/60ml nuoc mam Vietnamese fish sauce

Marinade:

3 cloves garlic, crushed pinch salt

1½ tbsp/20g sugar

4 tbsp /60ml nuoc mam

1. Toss chicken in flour to coat. Shake off excess flour and set aside.

2. Heat oil in a large, nonstick frying pan over a medium heat and cook chicken in batches, turning frequently, for 10 minutes or until brown on all sides. Remove chicken from pan and drain on absorbent kitchen paper.

3. Add garlic, onions or shallots, and bacon to pan and cook, stirring, for 5 minutes or until onions are golden. Return chicken to pan, stir in broth and wine and bring to the boil. Reduce heat, cover, and simmer, stirring occasionally, for 1¼ hours or until chicken is tender.

   Add mushrooms and black pepper to taste and cook for 10 minutes longer.

Ingredients

4½lb/2kg chicken pieces

½ cup/2oz/60g seasoned flour

2 tbsp/30ml olive oil

2 cloves garlic, crushed

12 pickling onions or shallots, peeled

Coq au Vin

8 slices bacon, chopped

1 cup/8fl oz/250ml chicken broth

3 cups/1¼ pt/750ml red wine

2 cups/8oz/250g button mushrooms

freshly ground black pepper

1   Pre-heat the oven to 350°F/180°C. Season the flour and place on a large plate, toss the meat until coated. Heat the oil in a large frying pan and cook the meat, over a medium heat, for 2-3 minutes each side, until browned (you will need to do this in two batches). Transfer the browned meat to a casserole dish, using a slotted spoon.

2.   Add the peppers to the frying pan and cook for 2 minutes. Add the tomatoes and bring to the boil.
Add these to the lamb and cook in the oven for 40 minutes or until the meat is tender. Meanwhile, mix all the ingredients for the gremolata together.

3.   Prepare the couscous according to package instructions, then fluff up with a fork. Heat the oil in a small frying pan and cook the onion over a medium heat for 10 minutes until golden brown. Add to the couscous and mix well.
Sprinkle the gremolata over the lamb casserole and serve with the couscous.

Lamb Casserole
with Couscous and Gremolata

Ingredients

sea salt and freshly ground black pepper

2 tbsp/60g all-purpose (plain) white flour

1lb 12oz/800g pack diced lamb, trimmed of any excess fat

2-3 tbsp/50-75ml extra virgin olive oil

1 yellow and 1 green bell pepper, deseeded and chopped

1¾ cups/14oz/400g chopped tomatoes

For the gremolata

1 garlic clove, minced

3 tbsp/75g minced parsley

grated rind of 1 lemon

For the couscous

1 cup/9oz/250g couscous

1 tbsp/15ml extra virgin olive oil

1 large onion, finely sliced

1. Toss beef in flour. Shake off excess and set aside. Heat half the oil in a large frying pan over a medium heat and cook beef in batches for 3-4 minutes or until brown. Place in a casserole dish.

2. Heat remaining oil in same pan, add onion and garlic and cook over a medium heat, stirring, for 4-5 minutes. Add leek and cook for 2-3 minutes longer. Add vegetables to casserole dish.

3. Add broth, wine, herbs, and black pepper to taste to pan and stirring, bring to the boil. Reduce heat and simmer until liquid reduces by half. Add broth mixture, bayleaf and orange rind, if using, to casserole dish and bake for 1½–2 hours at 420°F/210°C or until beef is tender.

4. Add zucchini (courgettes), sweet potato, and parsnip, and bake for extra 30 minutes or until vegetables are tender.

Ingredients

2½ lb/1 kg chuck or blade steak, trimmed of all visible fat and

cubed

½ cup/2oz/60g seasoned flour

¼ cup/2fl oz/60ml olive oil

1 onion, chopped

1 clove garlic, crushed

1 leek, sliced

2 cups/16fl oz/500 ml beef broth

Daube of Beef

1 cup/8fl oz/250ml red wine

1 tsp/5g dried mixed herbs

freshly ground black pepper

1 bayleaf

few thin strips orange rind (optional)

2 zucchini (courgettes), sliced

1 large sweet potato, chopped

1 parsnip, sliced

one-pot

Place a layer of potato slices, overlapping slightly, in the bottom of an ovenproof casserole dish. Arrange half the lamb slices and half the kidneys on top. Place another potato layer on top; then place remaining slices and kidneys on top. Finish with a layer of potatoes.

Combine cornstarch with ¼ cup/2fl oz/50ml cold water, and add the broth. Pour this into the casserole. Add the garlic, parsley, wine, rosemary, and pepper.

Cover and bake in a moderate oven for 3 hours. Remove lid and pour in melted butter, return to oven, bake for a further 20 minutes.

Lamb Hotpot

Ingredients

1 lb/500g washed potatoes, peeled and sliced into ¼ in/½cm thick rounds

1 lb/500g lamb fillets, cut into ½ in/1cm thick slices

8 lamb's kidneys, cut in half, crosswise, soaked in cold water for 30 minutes, drained

1 tbsp/15g cornstarch

1 cup/8fl oz/250ml meat broth

4 cloves garlic, crushed

2 tbsp/60g chopped fresh parsley

½ cup/4fl oz/125ml white wine

2 tsp/10g dried rosemary

1 tsp/5g cracked black pepper

2 tbsp/1oz/60g melted butter

1. Heat butter in a wide saucepan. Add the drumsticks a few at a time and brown lightly on all sides. Remove to a plate and brown the remainder.

2. Add green onions (scallions) and sauté for one minute. Stir in chopped dill. Add lemon juice. Return drumsticks to saucepan, sprinkle with salt and pepper.

3. Arrange the carrots over the drumsticks. Add water and bouillon cube. Bring to a simmer, reduce the heat, cover, and simmer for 40 minutes or until tender.

4. Remove drumsticks and carrots with a slotted spoon and arrange on a heated platter. Blend the cornstarch with the water, stir into the juices remaining in the pan. Stir over heat until sauce boils and thickens. Pour over drumsticks and carrots. Serve immediately with crusty bread.

Ingredients

2 tbsp/30g butter

2½ lb/1 kg chicken drumsticks

1 cup/3oz/90g chopped green onions (scallions)

3 tbsp/45g finely chopped dill

¼ cup/2fl oz/60ml lemon juice

Drumsticks in Dill Sauce

½ tsp/2.5g salt

¼ tsp/1.25g white pepper

1 bunch carrots, peeled

2 cups/16fl oz/500ml water

1 chicken bouillon cube

2 tbsp/50g cornstarch

2 tbsp/30ml water

one-pot

1. Preheat oven to 340°F/170°C. Trim lamb fillets of any fat, and remove silver skin. Butterfly lamb fillets and pound lightly to flatten. Drain lychees, reserve juice. Insert a pecan between 2 lychees, place onto 1 lamb fillet, roll up and secure with toothpicks. Repeat with the remaining lamb.

2 Brown lamb in nonstick frying pan. Transfer to large casserole dish. Heat butter in frying pan and sauté the onion. Add cornstarch blended with ¼ cup/2fl oz/50ml reserved juice, broth, and wine, bring to boil. Season to taste. Pour sauce over lamb, and cover the pan. Place vegetables in a separate Dutch oven or casserole dish with a little water, cover.

3. Cook lamb and vegetables in oven 30 minutes. Cook noodles according to package directions. Remove toothpicks from lamb, and serve with vegetables and noodles. Garnish with extra lychees and pecans.

Lychee Lamb

Ingredients

12 boneless lamb steaks, trimmed

1lb/565g canned or fresh, peeled lychees

4 tbsp/2oz/50g pecans

2 tsp/10g butter

1 onion, sliced

¼ cup/1oz/25g cornstarch

1 cup/8 fl oz/250ml chicken broth

1 cup/8 fl oz/250ml white wine

13oz/400g yellow baby squash

1¼ cups/9½ oz/300g green beans, topped and tailed

2 cups/8oz/250g shell or spiral noodles

1. Remove tentacles, intestines, and ink sac from octopus. Cut out the eyes and beak. Remove skin and rinse well.

2. Place octopus in a large saucepan, cover and simmer for 15 minutes. Drain off any juices and set aside to cool slightly.

3. Heat oil in a saucepan and cook shallots for 2-3 minutes. Add garlic and octopus and cook for 4-5 minutes. Pour wine into pan and cook over medium heat, until almost all the wine has evaporated.

4. Combine broth, tomatoes, lemon rind, pepper, and coriander. Cover and simmer gently for 1½ hours until octopus is tender.

Baby Octopus in Red Wine

Ingredients

2 lb/1 kg baby octopus

3 tbsp/45ml polyunsaturated oil

6 shallots, chopped

2 cloves garlic, crushed

½ cup/4fl oz/125ml dry red wine

½ cup/4fl oz/125ml chicken broth

1¾ cups/14oz/440g canned tomatoes, undrained and mashed

1 tsp/5g grated lemon rind

freshly ground black pepper

2 tbsp/30g finely chopped coriander

1. Fry bacon in a nonstick frying pan over moderate heat. Transfer to a large saucepan. Add oil to frying pan and sauté garlic, onion, bell pepper, and ham for 3 minutes. Stir in peas, cook for a further 2 minutes.

2. Transfer mixture to a large saucepan. Add the bacon. Stir mixture over moderate heat. Stir in broth, cook for 5 minutes. Stir in rice and cook for a further 5 minutes.

3. Blend or process ricotta cheese with yogurt until smooth, stir into rice mixture, and cook until heated through. Serve immediately.

Ingredients

1 cup/8oz/250g chopped bacon

2 tsp/10ml polyunsaturated oil

2 cloves garlic, crushed

1 onion, peeled and chopped

1 red bell pepper, seeded, finely chopped

2 cups/1 lb/450g roughly chopped, thickly sliced lean ham

Ham and Rice Casserole in Yogurt

1 cup/8oz/250g frozen peas, thawed

¾ cup/6fl oz/175ml broth

1½ cups/12oz/350g cooked, white, long grain rice

⅓ cup/ cooked wild rice

1 cup/8 oz/250g ricotta cheese

1 cup/8fl oz/250ml plain low fat yogurt

one-pot

45

1. Preheat the oven to 325°F/160°C. Heat half the oil in a large Dutch oven or flameproof casserole, add the onion, and cook for 5 minutes. Add half the steak and kidney and fry over a high heat, stirring, for 6 minutes or until browned. Keep warm. Fry the remaining meat, adding more oil if necessary.

2 Return all the meat to the dish, add the flour, and stir for 2 minutes. Add the tomato paste, Worcestershire sauce, broth, lemon rind, herbs, and salt and pepper. Bring to the boil, stirring, then cover.

3. Transfer to the oven. After 1½ hours, stir in the mushrooms, and a little water if needed. Cook for 35 minutes more. Meanwhile, roll out the dough and cut into 4 x 4½in/12cm circles. Transfer to a baking sheet.

4. Remove the casserole from the oven. Increase the oven temperature to 400°F/200°C. Place the casserole over a very low heat on the stove top. Keep covered but stir occasionally. Bake for 20 minutes or until golden brown. Top each pastry circle with the steak and kidney. Garnish with herbs.

Steak and Kidney Puffs

Ingredients

4 tbsp peanut oil

1 onion, minced

1lb 2oz/500g braising steak, trimmed of excess fat and cubed

12oz/350g pig's kidney, halved, cores removed, then cut into ½in/1cm pieces

3 tbsp/45g all-purpose (plain) flour

1 tbsp/15ml tomato purée

2 tsp/10ml Worcestershire sauce

1¾ cups/14fl oz/400ml beef broth

1 lemon, rind grated

2 tbsp minced fresh parsley, plus extra to garnish

1 tsp/5g dried mixed herbs

salt and black pepper

⅔ cup/5oz/150g baby button mushrooms

13oz/375g pack ready-rolled puff dough

fresh rosemary sprigs to garnish

1. Heat the oil in a large heavy-based saucepan, then add the garlic, chili flakes, if using, onions, eggplant (aubergine), zucchini (courgettes), and fennel. Stir well, and cook, covered, for 10 minutes, stirring often, or until the vegetables have softened.

2. Add the yellow pepper, tomatoes, lemon juice, sugar, oregano, and seasoning to the onion mixture. Simmer, uncovered, for 10 minutes or until all the vegetables are tender, stirring occasionally.

Ratatouille in Fresh Tomato Sauce

Ingredients

3 tbsp/45ml olive oil

2 cloves garlic, sliced

¼ tsp chili pepper flakes (optional)

2 red onions, sliced

1 large eggplant (aubergine), cut into

½in/1cm cubes

2 zucchini (courgettes), cut into

½in/1cm cubes

1 fennel bulb, cut into ½in/1cm cubes

1 yellow pepper, deseeded and

cut into ½in/1cm cubes

6 plum tomatoes, chopped

½ lemon, juice squeezed

1 tbsp/15g soft light or dark

brown sugar

1 tsp/5g dried oregano

black pepper

1. Preheat the oven to 400°F/200°C. You will need 6 x 2-cup/16fl oz/500ml capacity ovenproof pie dishes.

2. Heat the oil in a large pot, add the onion, and cook over a medium heat for 5 minutes or until golden. Add the garlic and the beef and cook for 5 minutes until the beef is browned.

3. Add the flour and tomato paste and cook for a further 2 minutes, stirring constantly. Stir in the red wine and broth and bring to the boil. Add the carrots, mushrooms, and chopped thyme. Reduce the heat, cover, and simmer for about 1 hour. Remove the lid and cook for a further 45 minutes until the beef is tender and the sauce is reduced and thickened. Stir in the parsley, transfer to a bowl, and allow the filling to cool completely.

4. Using the top of a pie dish as a guide, cut 6 circles from the dough, about 2cm/1in larger than the dish. Spoon the cooled filling into the dishes. Brush the edges of each pastry circle with a little water then cover the dishes with it, dampened side down, pressing the pastry to the side of the dish to seal. Cut a small cross in the top of each pie, insert a sprig of thyme and lightly brush with milk.

5. Bake for 20-25 minutes or until the pastry is crisp and golden and the filling is hot. Serve the pies with mashed potato and steamed green beans.

Ingredients

2 tsp/10ml peanut oil

1 large onion, chopped

2 cloves garlic, crushed

2¼lb/1 kg chuck steak, trimmed of all fat and cubed

2 tbsp/30g all-purpose (plain) flour

2 tbsp/30g low-sodium salt

1 tbsp/15ml tomato paste

1¾ cups/13fl oz/375ml red wine

Individual Beef and Red Wine Pies

1¾ cups/375ml low-sodium beef stock

2 carrots, thinly sliced

2 cups/7 oz/200g Portobello (chestnut) mushrooms, quartered

2 tbsp/30g fresh thyme, chopped

2 tbsp/30g fresh parsley, chopped

2 sheets puff dough, defrosted

4 sprigs thyme

1 tbsp/15ml low-fat milk

1   To make the rosemary mash, remove the leaves from the rosemary sprig. Place rosemary leaves and oil in a small saucepan over a low heat. Heat until warm. Remove pan from heat. Set aside to allow the flavors to develop. If possible do this several hours in advance, the longer the leaves can steep in the oil the more pronounced the flavor. Boil or microwave potatoes until tender. Drain well. Add milk and rosemary oil. Mash them together. Season with white pepper and lemon juice to taste. Keep warm or reheat just prior to serving.

2. Heat the oil in a large, deep-sided nonstick frying pan over a medium heat. Add leek and garlic. Cook, stirring, for 1-2 minutes or until soft. Add oregano, mushrooms, and celery. Cook, stirring, for 2-3 minutes. Stir in tomato paste. Cook for 3-4 minutes or until it becomes deep red and develops a rich aroma.

3   Stir in zucchini, tomatoes, and wine. Bring to the boil. Reduce heat. Simmer, stirring occasionally, for 5 minutes or until mixture starts to thicken.

4. Add fish. Cook for 6 minutes or until fish is just cooked (take care not to overcook or the fish will fall apart). Stir the basil and parsley into the fish.

5. To serve, place a mound of mash on each serving plate and top with fish stew. Accompany with a green salad or steamed green vegetables of your choice.

Rich Fish Stew
on Rosemary Mash

Ingredients

2 tsp/10ml olive oil

1 leek, chopped

1 clove garlic, crushed

1 tsp/5g ground oregano

4 flat mushrooms, sliced

1 stalk celery, sliced

1 tbsp/15g low-sodium tomato paste

2 zucchini (courgettes), sliced

1¾ cups/14oz/400g canned, diced tomatoes

½ cup/4 fl oz/125ml dry white wine

1¼ lb/500g firm white fish fillets (e.g. red snapper, ling, sea-bass, or cod)

1 tbsp/15g chopped fresh basil

1 tbsp/15g chopped fresh parsley

Rosemary Mash

1 sprig fresh rosemary

2 tsp/10ml olive oil

2 large potatoes, chopped

¼ cup/60ml low-fat milk, warmed

ground white pepper

lemon juice, optional

1. Preheat oven to 350°F/180°C. Trim beef of excess fat, cut it into 1in/3cm cubes, and toss in sufficient flour to coat. Heat oil in deep saucepan or Dutch oven and brown beef well.

2. Stir in tomatoes, corn, and Worcestershire sauce. Transfer to an ovenproof casserole dish. Cover and bake 2 hours, stirring occasionally. Remove casserole, increase heat 440°F/220°C.

3. Boil potatoes until soft. Drain and mash with egg, season to taste. Pipe swirls of potato onto greased cookie sheet. Bake at 15-20 minutes or until golden.

4 Meanwhile, steam or microwave cauliflower and broccoli 8-10 minutes.

5. Serve beef casserole with duchess potatoes, cauliflower, and broccoli.

Hearty Beef
Casserole with Duchess Potatoes

Ingredients

1½ lb/750g lean chuck steak

2-3 tbsp/30–45g all-purpose flour

1 tbsp/15ml olive oil

1¾ cups/14oz/420g canned tomatoes, undrained

2 cups/8oz/500g canned corn kernels, undrained

1 tbsp/15ml Worcestershire sauce

4 large potatoes, peeled and diced

1 egg, beaten

1½ cups/10oz/300g cauliflower flowerets

1½ cups/10oz/300g broccoli flowerets

1 Trim the fat from the chuck steak. Cut into large cubes. Peel and slice the carrots and onions. Heat a large heavy-based saucepan, add butter or oil, and a third of the beef. Toss to brown well on all sides over high heat. Remove and brown the remainder in 2 batches. Add the sliced carrot and onions and sauté until the onion is transparent.

2. Return all meat to saucepan and sprinkle with the flour over the entire surface. Add the garlic, dill, nutmeg, salt, pepper, and beef broth. Bring to the boil over high heat, stirring and scraping the sediment. Cover, reduce heat to low, cover, and simmer for 1½ hours.

3. Add dried fruits, mint, and coriander. Cover and simmer 30 minutes more or until meat is tender. Remove to a heated serving dish. Sprinkle with crushed walnuts and orange juice.

Ingredients

2½ lb/1kg thick-cut chuck steak

3 large carrots

3 medium onions, thinly sliced

2 tbsp/30ml butter or oil

2 tbsp/30ml all-purpose (plain) flour

2 cloves garlic, crushed

1 tsp/5g chopped fresh dill or ½ tsp/2.5g dried dill

½ tsp/2.5g nutmeg, grated or ground

salt and freshly ground black pepper

Jarkoy

1½ cups/12fl oz/350ml rich beef broth

½ cup/4oz/125g dried apricots

½ cup/4oz/125g dried peaches, cut in quarters

½ cup/4oz/125g pitted prunes

1 tsp/5g chopped mint

1 tbsp/15g chopped coriander

½ cup/2oz/50g walnuts, crushed

¼ cup/2 fl oz/60ml orange juice

one-pot

1. To make the marinade, place onion, macadamias, ginger, yogurt, and lime juice in a food processor. Process to combine. Stir in coriander, cardamom, and black pepper.

2 Place lamb in a non-reactive dish. Pour the marinade over it. Toss to coat. Cover and marinate in the refrigerator overnight.

3. Transfer meat mixture to a heavy-based saucepan. Stir in raisins and evaporated milk. Place pan over a medium heat. Bring to the boil, then cover the pan and reduce the heat to low. Cook, stirring occasionally for 1½ hours.

4 Remove cover. Cook, stirring occasionally, for 30-40 minutes longer or until meat is tender and sauce is thick. Add a little water during cooking, if necessary.

5 Serve with cooked rice and steamed vegetables of your choice.

Slow-cooked Lamb and Macadamias

Ingredients

1lb 5oz/600g boneless leg of lamb,

trimmed of visible fat, cut in 1in/3cm cubes

⅓ cup/3 tbsp/50 g raisins

⅔ cup/6½ fl oz/150ml evaporated skim milk

Spicy Yogurt Marinade

1 white onion, diced

50g/⅓ cup ground unsalted macadamias

1-2 cm piece fresh ginger, chopped

½ cup/4fl oz/125g low-fat natural yogurt

2 tsp/10ml lime or lemon juice

3 tsp/15g ground coriander

2 tsp/10g ground cardamom

½ tsp/2.5g freshly ground black pepper

1. Heat oil, add onions, and mushrooms. Cook until tender and remove from pan. Blend flour with oil lining the pan. Add seasonings, fry for 2 minutes then add milk gradually.

2. Cook oysters in their own liquor until edges curl. Add oysters and liquor to mixture. Add mushrooms, onion, and eggs then stir in sherry. Turn into greased casserole and bake at 400°F/200°C for 15 minutes. Serve on toast or pastry shells.

Ingredients

6 tbsp/90ml oil

½ small onion, sliced

1 cup/4oz/115g fresh mushrooms, sliced

4 tbsp/60g all-purpose (plain) flour

1 tsp/5g salt

Oyster Casserole

1 tsp/5g paprika

dash of cayenne

2 cups/16fl oz/500ml milk

2 dozen raw oysters, with their juice

3 hard-boiled eggs, sliced

2 tbsp/30ml cooking sherry

one-pot

1. Heat butter and oil in a large saucepan. When butter is foaming, add pork, and brown on all sides.

2. Add milk, pepper to taste and bring to the boil. Reduce heat to low, cover and cook for 1½-2 hours or until pork is cooked. Brush pork occasionally with milk during cooking.

3. At the end of cooking time, milk should have coagulated and browned in bottom of pan. If this has not occurred, remove the lid, and bring liquid to the boil. Boil until it has browned.

4. Remove meat from pan and set aside to cool slightly. Remove string from pork, cut into slices, and arrange on a serving platter. Set aside to keep warm.

5. Remove any fat from pan, stir in water and bring to the boil, scraping residue from bottom of the pan. Strain and spoon pan juices over pork to serve.

Ingredients

1oz/30g butter

1 tbsp/15ml vegetable oil

2 lb/1kg boneless pork loin, rolled and tied

2 cups/16fl oz/500ml milk

freshly ground black pepper

3 tbsp/45ml warm water

Pork Braised in Milk

one-pot

1. Brown small quantities of diced lean beef in hot oil in a large deep pan. Add onions, bell pepper, and mushrooms. Cook until onions are well browned.

2. Stir in tomatoes, wine, olives, fresh herbs, bayleaves, and pepper to taste. Cover and simmer on a low heat for 1½-2 hours or until the meat is tender.

3. Stir occasionally. Blend cornstarch in a little cold water. Stir the mixture into the casserole and stir until thickened. Adjust seasonings to taste.

4. Serve with new potatoes and steamed greens.

Beef Provençal

Ingredients

3lb/1½kg diced lean beef

1 tbsp/15ml oil

2 onions, sliced

1 red bell pepper

1 green bell pepper

2 cups/8oz/250g button mushrooms

3½ cups/1lb 12oz/800g canned tomatoes

½ cup/4fl oz/125ml red wine

½ cup/4fl oz/125ml black olives, pitted

2 tbsp/30g chopped fresh herbs
(basil, oregano, marjoram and sage)

2 bayleaves

dash of freshly ground pepper

¼ cup/2 tbsp/30g cornstarch

salt to taste

1. Brown the pork over high heat in a nonstick frying pan. Stir in garlic, onion, and salt. Cook for 5 minutes. Stir in the broth, simmer for 1½ hours.

2. Heat oil in a large, nonstick frying pan and sauté the bell pepper, celery, and carrots over high heat for 2 minutes.

3. Stir into meat casserole mixture, add tomatoes, chili pepper, mustard seeds, pepper, coriander, and lime juice; bring to the boil quickly and serve.

Ingredients

13 oz/400g pork fillet, cut into ¾ in/2cm cubes

2 cloves garlic, crushed

1 onion, peeled and finely chopped

¼ tsp/1.25g salt

4 cups/1¾ pints/1 l light broth

1 tbsp/15ml polyunsaturated oil

1 red bell pepper, seeded, cut into batons

1 cup/8oz/250g chopped celery

Pork Casserole

1 large carrot, cut into batons

1 cup/8oz/250g canned tomatoes, roughly chopped

1 tsp/5g finely chopped mild chili pepper

2 tsp/10g yellow mustard seeds

2 tsp/10g cracked black peppercorns

2 tbsp/30g chopped fresh coriander (cilantro)

2 tbsp/30ml freshly squeezed lime juice

one-pot

1. Heat a little of the oil over high heat in a deep-sided pan. Fry onion and garlic for 1-2 minutes. Remove and put aside.

2. Heat a little more oil on high. Brown beef in small batches, removing each batch before adding next.

3. Return beef and onion to pan. Add remaining ingredients, stirring to combine.

4. Cover and simmer gently for 1-1½ hours for blade or round, 1½-2 hours for chuck or shin. Stir occasionally. Season to taste. If curry needs thickening, boil with lid off for 10-15 minutes. Serve with rice, yogurt, and cucumber, banana, coconut, and slices of lime.

Spicy Beef with Lime Pickle

Ingredients

1½ lb/750g lean beef, diced-round, blade, or

chuck beef

1 tbsp/15ml canola (rapeseed) oil

1 onion, chopped

2 tsp/10g garlic, crushed

1 tbsp/15ml lime pickle

1 tbsp/15ml sambal oelek

(Indonesian hot chili paste)

1 cup/8fl oz/250ml beef broth

1. Thaw scallops if frozen. Wash scallops and drain well. Simmer scallops in boiling water. Drain. Sauté onions. Add soup, milk, curry, pepper, and half of the cheese. Stir until cheese melts.

2. Preheat the oven to in 425°F /215°C oven. Slice scallops and add to soup mix along with asparagus. Dip bread cubes in melted butter and add them. Sprinkle with remaining cheese. Bake for 15 minutes or until golden.

3. Remove from oven and sprinkle with chopped parsley and lemon rind prior to serving

Ingredients

18oz/500g scallops

¼ cup/2oz/50g chopped onions

1 cup/8fl oz/250ml cream of mushroom soup

½ cup/4fl oz/125ml milk

½ –1 tsp/2.5–5g curry powder

¼ tsp/1.25g pepper

Scallop Casserole

1 cup/8oz/250g shredded cheese

1 bunch asparagus, cut into 2in/4cm lengths

2 tbsp/1oz/30g melted butter

1 cup/4oz/125g bread cubes

parsley

1 lemon, rind grated

one-pot

1. Preheat the oven to 350°F/180°C. Combine the flour, mustard, and pepper, and coat the beef in the mixture. Heat 2 tbsp/30ml oil in a heavy-based frying pan. Fry a third of the beef for 3-4 minutes, until browned. Transfer to an ovenproof dish and fry the rest of the beef in 2 more batches.

2. Add another tbsp of oil to the pan, then fry the onions for 5 minutes. Add the garlic and cook for 2 minutes. Stir in the Guinness, Worcestershire sauce, herbs, and sugar, and simmer for 2-3 minutes. Pour the mixture over the beef, then cover and cook in the oven for 2 hours. Remove the beef and increase the oven temperature to 375°F/190°C. Fry the mushrooms in the rest of the oil. Stir into the beef, then transfer to a 6x8in/15x20cm pie dish.

3. Sift together the flour and ½ tsp/2.5g of the salt, then add the thyme and pepper. Stir in the suet and bind with 10-12 tbsp/150-200ml water to form a soft dough. Roll it out, dampen the edges of the dish, and cover with the pastry. Trim, then make a small slit in the center. Bake for 30-40 minutes, until golden.

Steak Pie with Guinness

Ingredients

3 tbsp/45ml all-purpose (plain) flour

1 tsp/5g English mustard powder

salt and black pepper

1lb 11oz/750g stewing beef, trimmed and cubed

4 tbsp/60ml vegetable oil

2 onions, sliced

2 cloves garlic, finely chopped

2 cups/500ml Guinness

2 tbsp/30ml Worcestershire sauce

2 bayleaves

1 tbsp/15g chopped fresh thyme

1 tsp/5g soft dark brown sugar

9oz/250g chestnut mushrooms, halved if large

For the pastry crust

9oz/250g self-raising flour

2 tsp chopped fresh thyme

4oz/125g shredded suet

one-pot

1. Preheat the oven to 325°F/160°C.

    Heat a large frying pan over a high heat and sear the lamb shanks in batches until browned all over. Transfer to an ovenproof casserole dish.

2. Add the tomatoes, red wine, bayleaf, thyme, and cinnamon stick. Cover and bake for 1 hour. Add the pumpkin, zucchini, apricots and prunes. Remove the lid and cook for 30 minutes longer or until the vegetables are soft and the lamb begins to come away from the bone.

3. Put the couscous in a large bowl, pour 2 cups/16fl oz/500ml boiling water over it and allow to stand for 10 minutes or until all the liquid is absorbed.

4. Serve the lambs shanks in deep bowls on top of the couscous and garnished with flaked almonds.

Ingredients

4 lamb shanks

1¾ cups/14oz/400g canned chopped tomatoes

1 cup/8fl oz/250ml red wine

1 bayleaf

6 sprigs fresh thyme

1 cinnamon stick

1 cup/8oz/250g pumpkin, cut into large pieces

Slow Simmered Lamb Shanks
with Couscous

2 zucchini (courgettes), cut into large pieces

8 dried apricots

8 dried prunes

1 cup/8oz/250g couscous

2 tbsp/30g flaked almonds, toasted

one-pot

75

For cooking in the microwave oven:

1. Marinate pork steaks in a shallow dish with garlic, herbs, Worcestershire and vinegar; turning to coat in mixture. Stand for ½ hour

2. Prick sausages and place in a shallow dish with sliced onion and bell pepper. Cover and microwave on HIGH for 7 minutes. Drain off any excess fat.

3. Cover pork steaks with vented plastic wrap and microwave for 13 minutes. Add sausage mixture, tomato pasta sauce, and beans, then cover and cook on HIGH another 5 minutes. Stand, covered, 3 minutes before serving.

Ingredients

1¼lb/500g pork leg steaks

1 tsp/5g crushed garlic

1 tbsp/15g chopped fresh sage and thyme

2 tbsp/30ml Worcestershire sauce

Spanish-style Pork Casserole

1 tbsp/15ml red wine vinegar

8oz/250g pork (chipolata) sausage links

1 medium sized onion, sliced

1½ cups/12oz/350g can tomato pasta sauce

1 cup/8oz/250g drained canned butter beans

1. Heat the oil in a large, nonstick frying pan over high heat. Add the oxtail, garlic, orange rind, and juice. Cook, stirring constantly, for 5 minutes. Pour over enough water to cover. Simmer gently for 2 hours, skimming the surface every 30 minutes.

2. Remove oxtail from stew, set aside, cover, and chill. Pour juices into a bowl, chill until fat sets on top. Peel off fat and discard. Return juice and meat to saucepan.

3. Stir in combined cornstarch and broth, orange marmalade, and Worcestershire sauce. Cook for a further 30 minutes. Just before serving, stir in pepper, orange segments, and green onions (scallions).

Orange Scented Oxtail Stew

Ingredients

1 tbsp/15ml olive oil

2½ lb/1¼ kg oxtail, cut into thick sections

3 cloves garlic, minced

⅓ cup/3½ fl oz/100ml orange juice concentrate

1 tbsp/15g finely grated orange rind

1½ tsp/7.5g cornstarch

½ cup/4fl oz/125ml beef broth

1 tbsp/15g orange marmalade

1 tbsp/15ml Worcestershire sauce

1 tsp/5g cracked black peppercorns

2 oranges, segmented

2 tbsp/20g minced green onions (scallions)

1   Trim excess fat from the chops. Wipe with kitchen paper.

Heat oil in a large, heavy-based saucepan or lidded skillet. Add onion and garlic and fry until golden over moderate heat. Remove onion with a slotted spoon, set aside.

2. Increase heat, and brown chops quickly on both sides, only 2 or 3 at a time. Remove to plate and drain almost all fat from the pan.

Add the curry powder and ginger to the hot saucepan and stir over heat until the fragrance emerges. Stir in the water, lifting the pan juices as you stir. Season with salt and pepper.

3. Return lamb and onion, cover and simmer for 1 hour. Add mixed dried fruits, brown sugar, and cinnamon stick and simmer for approximately 1 hour, until lamb is very tender. Add more water during cooking if necessary.

4. Remove chops to a hot serving platter. Stir yogurt into the sauce (if desired) and pour sauce over the chops. Serve with boiled rice.

Ingredients

6 forequarter lamb chops (around 1lb 14oz/850g)

1 tbsp/15ml oil

1 large onion, finely chopped

1 clove garlic, crushed

1½ tbsp/20g Madras-style curry powder

½ tsp/2.5g ground ginger

Sweet Lamb Chop Curry

2 cups/16fl oz/500ml water

salt and pepper

¾ cup/6oz/175g mixed dried fruits

1 tsp/5g brown sugar

½ cinnamon stick

½ cup/4fl oz/125ml plain yogurt (optional)

one-pot

1. Heat the olive oil in a large, nonstick frying pan over moderate heat. Add onions, bacon, garlic, and pepper, cook for 2 minutes. Add veal and stir constantly over moderately high heat until browned.

2. Transfer mixture to a large ovenproof dish, pour over combined broth, wine, and tomatoes. Stir in the flour mixture and bake, covered, in a moderate oven for 1½ hours, stirring every 30 minutes.

3. Heat butter in a medium, nonstick frying pan over moderate heat, add mushrooms, nutmeg, and sauté until cooked and browned. Stir into casserole and return to oven and cook for a further 1 hour or until veal is tender. Stir in the sour cream just before serving.

Veal and Mushroom Casserole

Ingredients

2 tbsp/30ml olive oil

2 onions, peeled and chopped

1 cup/8oz/250g chopped bacon

2 cloves garlic, crushed

¼ tsp/1.25g cayenne pepper

3lb/1½ kg lean stewing veal, cut into ¾ in/2 cm chunks

2½ cups/1 pint/1.25l chicken broth

¾ cup/6fl oz/175ml white wine

½ cup/4oz/125g chopped canned tomatoes

¼ cup/1oz/25g all-purpose (plain) flour, dissolved to a paste with

⅓ cup/3½fl oz/100ml cold water

2 tbsp/10z/25g butter

3 cups halved button mushrooms

½ tsp/2.5g ground nutmeg

¼ cup/2fl oz/50ml sour cream

1   Heat the oil in a large heavy-based saucepan, then add the onion, garlic, red pepper, and celery, and cook gently for 10 minutes or until softened.

2.   Stir in the tomatoes, chili, cayenne, paprika, and thyme and heat through for 1-2 minutes to release the flavors. Stir in the turkey strips and mushrooms, then cover the pan and cook gently for 30 minutes, stirring occasionally, until the turkey is cooked through and tender.

Ingredients

1 tbsp/15ml olive oil

1 onion, chopped

2 cloves garlic, chopped

1 red bell pepper, seeded and chopped

2 sticks celery, chopped

1¾ cups/400g can chopped tomatoes

1 tsp/5g chili powder

Turkey and Mushroom Casserole

large pinch of cayenne pepper

1 tsp/5g paprika

½ tsp/2.5g dried thyme

1lb/450g quick-cook turkey steaks, cut into strips

1cup/4oz/125g button mushrooms, sliced

1. Heat oil in a large, nonstick frying pan over high heat. Add veal chunks and sear well on all sides. Reduce heat to moderate, stir in onions, garlic, mushrooms, and pine nuts, cook, stirring constantly until pine nuts are golden. You may like to reserve 1 tbsp/15g pine nuts to garnish.

2   Add wine and basil to the frying pan, simmer gently for 5 minutes, scraping up browned bits from the bottom.

3   Stir in tomatoes, tomato paste, sugar, Worcestershire sauce, and chutney. Cover and simmer mixture gently for 1½ hours or until veal is tender. Serve sprinkled with mozzarella shavings.

Ingredients

2 tbsp/30ml olive oil

2½ lb/1 kg nut of veal, trimmed, cut into ¾ in/2 cm cubes

2 onions, peeled and roughly chopped

4 cloves garlic, finely chopped

2 cups/8oz/250g small button mushrooms

⅓ cup/3½oz/100g pine nuts

1 cup/8fl oz/250ml white wine

Veal Casserole in Tomato Basil Sauce

2 tsp/5g dried basil

3¾ cups/1lb 14oz/850g cans peeled tomatoes, chopped

3 tbsp/45ml tomato paste

½ tsp/2.5g brown sugar

2 tbsp/30ml Worcestershire sauce

1 tbsp/15ml sweet fruit chutney

1 cup/250g/8oz shredded mozzarella cheese

one-pot

1. Heat the oil in a large saucepan over high heat, add the lamb and brown all over. Add the onion, garlic, turmeric, coriander, cardamon, tomato paste, and sambal oelek and cook, stirring constantly, for a further 3 minutes.

2. Add the wine, bring to the boil, and reduce the heat. Add tomatoes and broth and stir in coconut cream. Simmer mixture gently for 1 hour.

3. Melt butter over moderate heat in a large frying pan. Add the bell pepper and sauté very lightly for 1 minute. Transfer to paper towels to drain. Serve lamb on rice, top with yogurt, and sautéed bell pepper.

Spicy Lamb and Yogurt Casserole

Ingredients

2 tbsp/30ml olive oil

1 lb/500g lean lamb, cut into ¾ in/2cm cubes

1 onion, peeled and minced

3 cloves garlic, crushed

2 tsp/10g ground turmeric

1 tbsp/15g ground coriander

1 tsp/5g ground cardamon

1 tbsp/15ml tomato paste

1 tsp/5g sambal oelek (chili paste)

¼ cup/2fl oz/30ml white wine

2 cups/1 lb/500g canned, peeled tomatoes, chopped

1½ cups/12fl oz/350ml broth

½ cup/4oz/125g coconut cream

2 tbsp/1oz/30g butter

½ cup/4oz/125g finely chopped bell pepper

¼ cup/2 fl oz/50ml plain yogurt

1. Preheat the oven to 350°F/180°C. Melt butter in a heavy flameproof casserole. Sauté onion, celery, and mushrooms, if using, for about 5 minutes. Add the chops and sauté, until they turn color. Add barley, stir, and add hot broth and tomatoes, including juice. Cover and bake for 1–1½ hours.

2. Check once or twice during cooking time and add more broth or water if barley is dry. Season to taste with salt and pepper. Before serving, sprinkle with chopped parsley and cheese.

Ingredients

4 tbsp/2oz/60g butter

1 onion, sliced

2 sticks celery, sliced

1 cup/4oz/125g mushrooms, sliced (optional)

1lb 10oz/750g lamb neck chops

1½ cups/12oz/350g pearl barley, washed and drained

Lamb and Barley Casserole

2 cups/16 fl oz/500ml hot broth

1¾ cup/14oz/400g canned peeled tomatoes

salt and freshly ground black pepper

4 tbsp/60g chopped parsley

2 tbsp/30g grated Parmesan cheese

1. Remove bones and cut lamb into large pieces, leaving any visible fat on the meat. In a large saucepan, cook lamb over low heat, stirring frequently for 10 minutes, or until it is no longer pink. Add onion and cook mixture over moderately low heat, stirring occasionally, until the onion is softened. Add tomatoes (breaking them up with a wooden spoon), potatoes, a pinch of salt and freshly ground pepper, and simmer the mixture, half-covered, stirring occasionally for 40 minutes or until lamb and potatoes are tender.

2. Add the herb mixture and cayenne, stirring, and simmer the stew for a further 4 minutes. Stir in the garlic and remove the stew from the heat. Let the stew stand, covered, for 5 minutes and season with salt and pepper before serving.

Ingredients

1lb 10oz/750g large lamb chops

1 large onion, chopped

1¾ cups/14oz/400g can peeled tomatoes, drained

2¼lb/1kg potatoes, peeled and cut into ½in/1.5cm pieces

salt and freshly ground pepper

Georgian Lamb Stew

½ cup/4 oz/125g coarsely chopped fresh coriander

leaves, mint leaves, basil leaves, dill sprigs,

and parsley leaves

½ tsp/2.5g cayenne pepper

4 cloves garlic

one-pot

1. Melt the butter or lard and chicken fat in a deep frying pan, add the chicken, and brown all over. Remove and keep warm.

   Add okra, onion, garlic, ham, and pepper to the pan and stir-fry until onion is soft.

2. Next, add the tomatoes, tomato paste, wine or broth, bayleaf, salt, pepper, and cayenne or Tabasco to taste.

3. Add chicken to pan, cover and simmer for 40 minutes, until chicken is tender. Sprinkle with chopped parsley and serve with boiled rice.

Chicken Gumbo

Ingredients

6tbsp/3oz/90g butter, or lard and chicken fat

6-8 chicken thighs, legs, or wings

2 cups/1lb/500g okra

1 large onion, minced

1 clove garlic, crushed

8 oz/250g ham, cut in one slice, then in cubes

1 red bell pepper, seeded and cubed

1½ cups/12oz/350g tomatoes, peeled and chopped

1 tbsp/15ml tomato paste

½ cup/4fl oz/125ml dry white wine or chicken broth and water

1 bayleaf

salt and freshly ground pepper

cayenne pepper or Tabasco sauce

2 tbsp/30g minced parsley

Index